Jimi Hendrix

by

Bruce Mann

AN ORION PAPERBACK

This is a Carlton Book

First published in Great Britain in 1994 by Orion Books Ltd,
Orion House, 5 Upper St Martin's Lane, London WC2H 9EA

A CIP catalogue record for this book is available from the British Library.

ISBN 1 85797 583 9

Edited, designed and typeset by Haldane Mason
Printed in Italy

THE AUTHOR
Bruce Mann is the pen name of a well-known British author, pop historian and musician.

PICTURE ACKNOWLEDGEMENTS
Photographs reproduced by kind permission of London Features International;
Pictorial Press /J. Cummins, /Tony Gale, /E. Landy, /Chuck Pulin, /Wertzell, /Vinnie Zussante;
Redferns /Billy Cox, /David Redfern; Rex Features.
Front cover picture: Pictorial Press

CONTENTS

Introduction

Jimi Hendrix was the most vital electric guitarist that this century has ever produced. While he did not owe his celebrity entirely to instrumental prowess, his whimsical elasticity, masterful technique and outright craziness on a left-handed Fender Stratocaster transformed a shy teenager from Seattle into one of the few pop icons of the Sixties to deserve the epithet "legendary".

He arrived in London in 1966 after years of criss-crossing North America as a jobbing accompanist to such as the Isley Brothers and Little Richard. British Top 10 smashes with 'Hey Joe', 'Purple Haze' and 'The Wind Cries Mary' set the Jimi Hendrix Experience on the path to the global success that was sealed by a show-stealing performance at 1967's Monterey Pop Festival. It was showmanship as much as fretboard fireworks that was to make Hendrix a hit at Woodstock, too, after 1968's *Electric Ladyland* topped the US album chart.

Wary of re-creating past glories, a spell as leader of the all-American Band of Gypsys preceded a mooted stage reunion with The Experience. With members from both outfits, he undertook some European dates in the summer of 1970, and was discussing a possible fusion with the cream of modern jazz musicians before his sudden death at the age of 27.

Jimi's records have gone on to sell many millions, with new compilations being released each year. His father, Al Hendrix, used the royalties to set up the Jimi Hendrix Memorial Foundation in 1971, to award scholarships to talented young musicians in Washington. The UK's *Sunday Times* obituary predicted that Hendrix would "probably soon slide out of pop's memory", but the 20th anniversary of Jimi Hendrix's passing was celebrated in 1990 with myriad retrospectives on record, film screenings, biographies and even a jeans commercial on TV. His name lives on.

Jimi Hendrix in 1967—a cult celebrity
about to become a household name.

CHAPTER 1

Key to the Highway

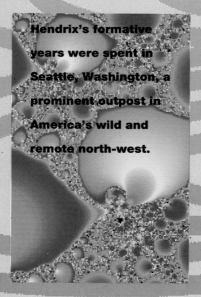

Hendrix's formative years were spent in Seattle, Washington, a prominent outpost in America's wild and remote north-west.

His great-great grandmother was a Cherokee princess, his grandfather was a Chicago policeman, and his grandmother was a dancer in a vaudeville troupe. His parents, Al and Lucille, were semi-professional dancers during the Thirties recession. They married just before Al Hendrix was drafted into the army to fight during the Second World War. As an army private, Al was in a detention stockade when Lucille, then barely 17, gave birth to Johnny Allen, eldest of their three sons, in Seattle's King County Hospital on November 27, 1942. In 1946, after the hostilities were over, Al renamed the boy James Marshall Hendrix (nicknamed Buster).

Al and Lucille's marriage was far from ideal, and Jimmy's brother Leon recalls a tempestuous atmosphere. "I was four, and Jimmy was ten. Every day was about the same. I'd wait for Jimmy to get home from school, and then we'd play outside. Mom would invite friends over and they'd drink. Then Dad would get mad. It happened over and over again—and so finally they got divorced after arguing about it for six years."

The brief marriage ended, with Al awarded custody of the children, when Jimmy was nine. An incidental figure during Jimmy's infancy at the best of times, his mother remarried but died of liver failure in 1958. Despite her irregular appearances in Jimmy's life, she was still his mother, and he was devastated by her death, though he hid his grief. She remained a presence in his life, and was to appear in his dreams, lyrics and interviews for many years.

Al resolved to ensure that Jimmy and his brothers, Leon and Joseph, were as comfortable as post-war economies, racial prejudice and his fluctuating means would allow. He kept the wolf from the door as best he could as a cleaner, mill-hand, market trader and petrol-pump attendant between periods of unemployment. As a result, the family moved several times, and the boys went to many different schools.

Jimmy was sound enough in most subjects at school, and displayed a flair for art and creative writing. Through both of these subjects, he revealed an obsession with astronomy that he never outgrew. Surprisingly, he was poor at music, perhaps because in those

> **"I was four, and Jimmy was ten. Every day was about the same. I'd wait for Jimmy to get home from school, and then we'd play outside. Mom would invite friends over and they'd drink. Then Dad would get mad. It happened over and over again—and so finally they got divorced after arguing about it for six years."**
>
> Leon Hendrix

Al Hendrix, Jimmy's father, was a semi-professional dancer during the Thirties.

9

distant days, it was taught virtually as a kind of mathematics.

Musical inspirations

Like most children of the 1950s, Jimmy was superficially thrilled by the metronomic clamour of Bill Haley and the Comets' 'Rock Around The Clock'. A more profound impression was made by Elvis Presley's hillbilly blues singing that the USA only dared televise from the waist up. Presley wasn't married and paunchy like Haley; garbed in his flash "cat" clothes, this "unspeakably untalented and vulgar young entertainer"—as a US TV guide described him—made adult flesh creep. Unlike Bill Haley, he made no apologies for his go-man-go onstage frolics, which involved hip-swivelling, doing the splits and rolling about as if he had a wasp in his pants.

Even more unhinged than Elvis

In 1957 Jimmy saw Elvis Presley in concert in Seattle.

was raving Little Richard—the "Georgia Peach"—beating hell out of a grand piano in *The Girl Can't Help It*, a pop movie that reached Seattle in 1957. Every week seemed to bring another wildman into *Billboard*'s Hot 100 record sales chart—like duckwalking Chuck Berry, Jerry Lee Lewis, a piano-pumping fireball from Louisiana, and crippled Gene Vincent, "The Screaming End".

Jimmy's growing record collection included all these and more. Later, he was attracted to Buddy Holly and impressed by the output of Motown (later, Tamla-Motown), a promising black record label from Detroit that, by 1960, had manoeuvred its first fistful of signings into the Hot 100.

Blues and gospel

The bedrock of both rock 'n' roll and soul were blues (and R&B) and—the other side of the coin—gospel music. Though he had ceased to be a communicant by the time he finished school, the gospel hymns that Jimmy had sung at the Pentecostal Church where the family worshipped had left their mark. More obviously telling, however, were the wickedly secular sounds of the blues. He grew particularly fond of Muddy Waters, Guitar Slim, Big Bill Broonzy and B. B.

Little Richard—the "Georgia Peach"—was one of Hendrix's early role models.

11

> "[Parachuting] is the most alone feeling in the world, and every time you jump, you're scared that maybe it won't open this time. Then you feel a tug on your collar and you see the air going sssssssh past your ears. That's when you begin to talk to yourself again."
>
> **Jimi Hendrix**

King. Their respective signature tunes, 'Hoochie Coochie Man', 'The Things I Used To Do', 'Key To The Highway' and 'Rock Me Baby' were to be part of Jimmy's basic repertoire after he taught himself guitar at the age of 16.

Muddy Waters left his mark on Jimmy's musical and composing style.

12

Apart from an unsatisfactory home-made creation, Jimmy's first stringed instrument was a ukelele, a wise choice, as his right hand was not yet big enough to shape guitar chords fully. One of the first tunes he mastered was 'Peter Gunn' as rendered in the "twangy" guitar picking of Duane Eddy. Acquiring an acoustic guitar, Jimmy proved to be a natural musician, and, by trial and error, he developed the naïve beginnings of a personal style.

Al managed to scrape up enough cash for a solid-body electric model. Supporting his son's new activity with unusual zest, Al bought himself a saxophone, which he took to honking in the evenings, while Jimmy vamped his handful of chords.

B. B. King's 'Rock Me Baby' was to be part of Jimmy's basic repertoire after he taught himself to play the guitar.

The Rocking Kings

By 1959, Jimmy was performing semi-professionally with the Rocking Kings, a local outfit who specialized in assembly-line pop laced with synchronized footwork. He played not one of the new electric models but the deeper octaves of an ordinary six-string.

Jimmy transferred to lead guitar—though most solos in those days were taken on a brash tenor saxophone—when he joined Thomas and the Tomcats in 1960. That same year he left school without graduating to work as a labourer for Al,

13

Billy Cox first met Hendrix in the army, and was to become not only a member of his band but also one of his greatest friends.

who was now a self-employed landscape gardener. But rather than wait for the draft, Jimmy volunteered in 1961 to do his national service in the 101st Airborne Division—the "Blue Angels"—as a parachutist. "It's the most alone feeling in the world," he later mused, "and every time you jump, you're scared that maybe it won't open this time. Then you feel a tug on your collar and you see the air going sssssssh past your ears. That's when you begin to talk to yourself again."

The King Kasuals

During basic training at Fort Campbell, Kentucky, Jimmy teamed up with other black recruits in the King Kasuals, a besuited R&B quintet who

entertained at functions in and around the base, sometimes playing as far away as Nashville, Tennessee. The King Kasuals' bass player was a Virginian named Billy Cox, and he and Jimmy became great friends. Mitch Mitchell later described Billy as "the nicest guy you could ever meet". Both were demobbed in summer 1962. Jimmy owed his discharge to injuries sustained during parachute training: "One day I caught my foot in the sky hook just as I was about to land, and broke my ankle. I told them I'd hurt my back too. Every time they examined me, I moaned. In the end, they let me get out."

Billy and Jimmy hawked a civilian edition of the King Kasuals round Nashville's R&B clubland. Bookings were so scarce for them that a temporary—and then permanent—disbandment was decided upon while they each found work elsewhere. Cox and Hendrix joined Bob Fisher and his Barnevilles, bottom on the bill of a package tour. On this 30-day jaunt, the Barnevilles provided accompaniment for Curtis Mayfield and the Impressions and the all-female Marvelettes, a Tamla-Motown act, then on the rebound from a *Billboard* chart-topper, 'Please Mr Postman'.

Lean times

Jimmy and Billy then went separate ways. Jimmy wintered in Vancouver, where he made

Curtis Mayfield was in the Impressions when Hendrix backed him in the early Sixties.

ends meet with a night spot residency backing vocalist Bobby Taylor. By the following March, he'd returned to Nashville to slip into a routine of two, maybe three bookings a week with a reconstituted King Kasuals, and less frequent stints playing behind visiting R&B/soul stars.

With no better prospects looming, Jimmy threw in his lot with "Gorgeous" George Odell, a blond-wigged bandleader and all-round showman with a silver-tongued talent for self-promotion. Yet, if Jimmy was expecting to soar swiftly to the very peaks of pop under Odell's wing, the next three years on back-to-back tours and one-night stands were to disillusion him. Sometimes, he and Odell worked not as musicians but as mere valets to singers or groups who'd been lucky enough to catch the lightning when some Svengali came by.

Jamming with the stars

There were frequent occasions when Jimmy couldn't resist removing his guitar from the potato sack that served as a case, and "sitting in" on

During the early Sixties, Jimmy adopted the stage name "Maurice James".

ad hoc get-togethers after the show. Henry Nash of the Upsetters was one of many struck by this raw talent. "I will never forget Jimmy loading his belongings on the bus. His guitar was wrapped in a potato sack. It had only five strings on it. Gorgeous George talked me into letting Jimmy sit in with the Upsetters. He played the entire night with only five strings to his guitar."

During a lull back in Nashville, one such occurrence centred on Albert King, a genuine and esteemed exponent of the electric blues guitar, Chicago style—simultaneously delicate and brutal. As King was also left-handed, Hendrix found the session particularly instructive, and he drank in King's terse, resonant technique, and his practice of using slack lower strings. That was the secret of King's agile bending, two at a time, of middle register "blue" notes.

As a measure of Jimmy's increasing confidence and ability, he'd even be invited—or just wander—on stage during shows. Such starstruck escapades were generally tolerated because Hendrix—who had by now adopted the stage name "Maurice James"—

rarely showed himself up. Soon, he was being engaged more often as a guitarist than as a dressing-room dogsbody. Beyond the main spotlight, he and the other hired hands bobbed

Hendrix serving his time as backing guitarist for an R&B band in New York, in 1964.

around in choreographed movements and identical costumes. Maurice-Jimmy had a long way to go yet, and the money wasn't brilliant—but at least he wasn't kicking his heels in Nashville any more. Nowadays, he was breathing the air around

As "Maurice James", Jimmy was a full-time member of Little Richard's Upsetters in 1965.

"He [Jimmy] began to dress like me, and he even grew a little moustache like mine. He had watched me work and just loved the way I wore these head-bands around my hair and how wild I dressed."

Little Richard

Once fans mistook Jimmy for Little Richard and demanded Richard's autograph from him.

big names like Jackie Wilson, Slim Harpo, the Supremes, Curtis Mayfield, Sam Cooke, Ike and Tina Turner—and Little Richard.

Little Richard

Of all the professional learning experiences Jimmy had on the road, it was working with Richard that was the most significant in terms of how Jimmy looked and conducted himself on the boards.

Constant replay of Bob Dylan albums opened Jimmy's ears to the possibilities of becoming a guitarist *and* singer.

just loved the way I wore these headbands around my hair and how wild I dressed." On one occasion, over-enthusiastic fans, spotting Jimmy's precarious pompadour and mistaking it for Little Richard's, cornered him, demanding Richard's autograph. Years later, the cover illustration on a bootleg Hendrix album depicted him at first glance as just like his former boss.

During the joyous gibberish of 'Good Golly Miss Molly', 'Keep A-Knockin', 'Jenny Jenny Jenny' or any other of his bombastic 12-bar smashes, the elder statesman of rock 'n' roll would stretch it out up to ten minutes, take it down easy, build the tension to raving panic and, finally, sweep into the wings, leaving 'em wanting more.

"He began to dress like me," recalled the narcissistic Richard, "and he even grew a little moustache like mine. He had watched me work and

Learning the hard way

Being confused with Little Richard was only a second-hand taste of stardom. The reality of a jobbing guitarist's working life in the mid Sixties was grim digs (if any), coats for blankets, long hours, virtually no sleep, and only junk food and amphetamines to keep him going. Under such

Like his hero Dylan, Hendrix had the look of a wandering minstrel.

sordid conditions, the spurious thrill of "going professional" gave way rapidly to stoic cynicism as the cash for each week's work ran out well before pay day.

For Jimmy, these interminable exercises in a kind of exhilarating drudgery were to have a lasting, beneficial effect. However hard-won his musicianship and stagecraft had been by 1966, they were perfected in readiness for what lay ahead.

Bright lights, big city

He was still Maurice James when his wanderings took him, by the beginning of 1964, to New York, his base for the next 18 months. It was almost a matter of course that Jimmy would be drawn to Greenwich Village. This vibrant beatnik district first intruded upon mass-market consciousness with Peter, Paul and Mary's 'Blowing In The Wind', an anti-war opus

After Hendrix became famous, his recordings with Curtis Knight were repromoted.

written by Bob Dylan, a regular performer at the Village's Gaslight club. Jimmy had been most enthusiastic about Dylan's early albums with their down-home intonation, untutored phrasing and eccentric breath control. He became even more captivated with Dylan after Dylan "went electric", around 1965. Constant replay of Dylan's records opened Jimmy's ears to the possibilities of becoming a guitarist and singer. If Dylan could get away with slovenly diction and gravelly ranting, so could he. So Jimmy —who had started writing songs partly to ease the tedium of the road—put his mind to Dylan-type creations.

Nobody of any importance, however, wanted to hear a home-made song by a jobbing guitarist called Maurice James. However much he dreamed of making his own music, it was business as usual, picking up work as a backing musician for tours, residencies, one-nighters and, more recently, recording sessions. For several months, Jimmy serviced the Isley Brothers, Cincinatti soul siblings, who were then milking the Beatles' rehash of their 1962 hit 'Twist And Shout'.

> **"I will never forget Jimmy loading his belongings on the bus. His guitar was wrapped in a potato sack. It had only five strings on it. Gorgeous George talked me into letting Jimmy sit in with the Upsetters. He played the entire night with only five strings to his guitar."**
>
> **Henry Nash of the Upsetters**

Upsetting with Little Richard

Jimmy re-enlisted with Little Richard in 1965 as a full-time member of his Upsetters. No longer quite the rank-and-file rhythm guitarist of the Gorgeous George days, Jimmy was permitted to take an occasional solo. As a satellite in Richard's stellar firmament—which now included a pair of belly dancers—it was incumbent upon him to ham it up during these big moments. As Richard hammered the ivories with his feet, buttocks and knees, so Jimmy trained himself to pick the strings with his teeth, and, for an extra bit of swagger, with anything else—he'd play his Fender Jazzmaster on the back of his neck, above his head or in the small of his back. Then he'd use the microphone stand or edge of an amplifier to create a bottleneck guitar effect.

As an Upsetter, he was heard on 'I Don't Know What You Got But It's Got Me', follow-up to 'Bama Lama Bama Loo', one of Richard's last *Billboard* Hot 100 entries in the US. He also made a television début on *Night Train*, a programme broadcast from Texas, before leaving Little Richard under something of a cloud. Allegedly, he was fired for deliberate defiance of his paymaster's rules about time-keeping and sitting in with other bands. Matters had come to a head when he missed the tour bus from New York to a show in Washington DC.

Squiring Curtis Knight

There was nothing more worthwhile in the offing, so he moved to a post in Curtis Knight and the Squires, a dance band with a moderately full calendar. They had an endearingly ragged dissimilarity to the slick Isley Brothers and to Little Richard's contrived splendour. Knight also had a recording contract through which he planted unfruitful feet in both the soul and mainstream pop camps. Jimmy was featured on many Knight recordings such as 'How Would You Feel', an A-side that borrowed much from Bob Dylan's 1965 million-seller, 'Like A Rolling Stone'.

Though the group might have slipped in its flop singles when playing the clubs, dancers reacted more positively to conveyor-belt Top 40 hits like 'Hang On Sloopy', 'Twist And Shout', 'Satisfaction', 'Midnight Hour', 'Daytripper', 'Land Of A Thousand Dances' and 'Wooly Bully'. For an audible gauge whereby performances could be measured against rival outfits, several bashes were recorded "live"—often with hand-held microphones—in varying degrees of fidelity. After Hendrix became famous, these and his studio efforts with Knight were re-promoted. But none of these songs was particularly successful in 1965, so Jimmy reverted from time to time to better-paid work behind people like King Curtis, Wilson Pickett, Percy Sledge, Joey Dee

> ## "I was the hottest guitarist on the block. I thought I was it. I went right across the street and saw him. That day, in front of my eyes, he burned me to death. I didn't even want to pick up a guitar for the next year."
>
> ### Mike Bloomfield

and the Starliters, and Sam and Dave from whom he was sacked for his "weird innovations".

Jimmy James and the Blue Flames

After a 1966 fortnight with Carl Holmes and his Commanders, Jimmy finally threw caution to the wind and formed his own unit. He considered calling it the Rainflowers, but settled for a name that would differentiate between the front man—

In 1966 Hendrix's pompadour grew out to a thick barbed-wire aureole like Bob Dylan's.

him—and the others. He was now Jimmy James and the group were the Blue Flames, the best known of whom were Al Kooper, the organist on Dylan's *Highway 61 Revisited* album, and Randy California, the second guitarist before returning to Los Angeles to be a mainstay of middle-league "progressive" band, Spirit.

Jimmy James and the Blue Flames' stamping ground was Greenwich Village clubland—principally, the Night Owl, the Café A Go-Go and, opposite the Gaslight, the Café Wha? Jimmy made an immediate impact on the club scene, eclipsing the local talent, such as Mike Bloomfield, who had played on *Highway 61 Revisited*. "I was the hottest guitarist on the block. I thought I was it. I went right across the street and saw him. That day, in front of my eyes, he burned me to death. I didn't even want to pick up a guitar for the next year."

Sometimes, there was a trip uptown to Ondine's on 59th Street, popular for its flattering lighting that made everyone look suntanned and fit. Ronnie Spector was one of the regulars, who often used to get up and sing with Hendrix. "We always had so much fun at Ondine's that we often wouldn't leave till dawn."

Wild man Hendrix

With extreme strategy the norm in today's rock, it may be difficult to appreciate how outrageous

Hendrix must have seemed at this time. His hair grown out to a thick barbed-wire aureole, he'd take the stage in garb that only the boldest would be seen dead in. A wanton dedication to pleasing himself rather than the paying customer culminated in a sweaty intensity as he seized songs like the Troggs' 'Wild Thing' by the scruff of the neck and wrung the life out of it. The idea was to make it—and every other non-original in the set—sound completely different to any other act's version.

Other showstoppers included Howlin' Wolf's 'Killing Floor'—an attack on armed discord between nations—and the semi-traditional 'Hey Joe'. Both were on a par with 'Louie Louie' and Them's 'Gloria' as fixtures in the repertoires of countless mid-Sixties "garage bands" throughout the world.

Whatever the number, Hendrix came on like an exaggerated composite of every guitarist and showman he'd ever admired. To this brew was added a transforming ingredient: Jimmy had found his voice at last. While he'd sung the odd lead vocal with Knight and the Squires, he was unaccustomed to keeping it up for an entire evening. Still, he proved equal to the challenge; learning that he could do, say, 'Midnight Hour' without losing any of Wilson Pickett's fervour.

He sang any-old-how in a droll, slurred, one-note husk, incapable of pitching far beyond his

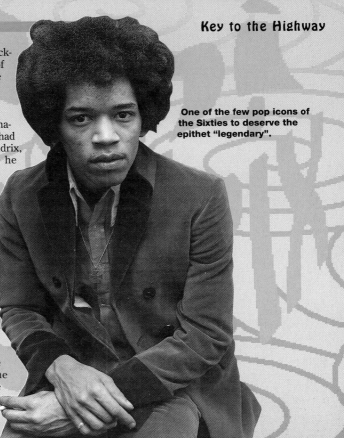

central octave without cracking. In context, the effect of spontaneity over expertise worked.

Creating a buzz
The greatest musical emphasis during the early Sixties had been on vocals, but Hendrix, effective singer though he turned out to be, owed most of his local celebrity to instrumental prowess. Twisting the heartstrings tighter than the most anguished wail from his larynx were his exquisite brushstrokes of fretboard inflexion on what was to become a trademark Fender Stratocaster. A fractional widening of vibrato during a sustained, shivering note could be as loaded as the most over-amplified chord during one of his Little Richard stunts. When he played the blues, even the

One of the few pop icons of the Sixties to deserve the epithet "legendary".

most uninvolved drinkers would fall silent with a mingling of awe and scepticism—as if he wasn't quite real. The bars weren't packed yet, but there was an intangible buzz in the air when he played. Jimmy's time was about to come.

Chas Chandler

It came in the stout form of Chas Chandler, bass guitarist with the Animals. As his group was on its farewell tour of the States, he had decided to diversify into behind-the-scenes branches of showbusiness for fun and profit. On the recommendation of Rolling Stone Keith Richards' girl-friend, Linda Keith, he "discovered" Hendrix during a casually cataclysmic performance in a half-empty Café Wha?

Chandler tuned into the mixture of epic vulgarity and passion as Hendrix walked his customary artistic tightrope without a safety net. When he sauntered off, Chas went straight backstage with an offer. If Jimmy agreed to come to England, Chandler—and business partner Mike Jeffery, the Animals' manager—would build a group round him, and procure a recording deal.

Jimmy had had his past disappointments. Though bemused by Chandler's overtures, he

Another chapter begins as Jimmy leaves New York to try his luck in London.

Hendrix with Chas Chandler, who became Jimmy's manager and record producer.

wasn't as nonchalantly indifferent to them as he may have appeared. The consolation of a moderately full workload within easy reach of his frowzy room in the Village was wearing thin. What did he have to lose by trying his luck in London? He agreed. Sinking into uneasy oblivion on the flight to Heathrow on September 23, 1966, Jimmy let himself be pushed in whatever direction fate, Chandler and Jeffery ordained.

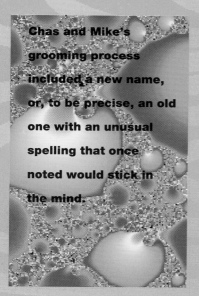

Chas and Mike's grooming process included a new name, or, to be precise, an old one with an unusual spelling that once noted would stick in the mind.

O n the agenda too were auditions for two musicians to make up the rest of "The Jimi Hendrix Experience". It was to be a trio with Hendrix, a bass guitarist and a drummer. As the very name of the group suggested, the latter two had to be a fluid complement to Jimi's playing and image. While they could cultivate distinct musical and stage personae, they were not to threaten their leader with any direct rivalry.

The new recruits

From an array of eager bass players, Chas and Jimi chose Noel Redding, a lead guitarist who—as Hendrix had been in the Rocking Kings—was persuaded to transfer to bass. As well as an unusual fretboard dexterity and owlish John Lennon spectacles, he was conspicuous for an Afro hairstyle vaguely like that of shock-headed Jimi.

Noel had been under the delusion that the vacancy was for a New Animal. Nevertheless, at a low ebb professionally, he was glad of whatever else was going. The alternative was the more secure anonymity of delivering milk in his native

Folkestone after four years of struggling with groups like the Lonely Ones and the Loving Kind.

The only one of Noel's old groups to endure was Screaming Lord Sutch and the Savages. Another who served under this godfather of

Above: As a member of the Loving Kind, Noel Redding played on the only single by Freddie, John Lennon's father.

Left: The Jimi Hendrix Experience make their début at London's Marquee in January 1967.

British horror rock was London drummer John "Mitch" Mitchell. His musical resumé was more impressive than Redding's. Even before turning professional, he'd been in Johnny Kidd and the Pirates, had played on Riot Squad singles, toured with the Kinks and, under console boffin Joe Meek, played with the latter-day Tornadoes. Later, after a short spell with the Pretty Things, he succeeded Jimmy Nicol in Georgie Fame and the Blue Flames (nothing to do with Hendrix's old band). Fame had just

John "Mitch" Mitchell drummed with Georgie Fame's Blue Flames among others before joining The Experience.

disbanded the group, and Mitch was looking for another opening when he was asked to try out for The Experience.

Aynsley Dunbar from John Mayall's Bluesbreakers was a close second, but Mitch landed the job because of his astonishingly

busy style; sometimes too quick for the eye to follow, it nevertheless maintained a brisk finesse and a precise backbeat.

The Experience in France

The new boys were broken in with a short tour of France as support act to Johnny Halliday and other Gallic pop luminaries. This is where the three really began to get to know each other. At their first live gig, Noel and Mitch were amazed at Jimi's brilliant showmanship and stunts with his guitar. They knew from practices that he was a great guitarist, but had never before seen him playing his guitar behind his head, with his teeth, under his knee, and more. And, as Mitch has been known to say, it wasn't just flashiness—he really did have the musician-ship to go with the performance.

During a 15-minute set, in which they were sometimes less prominent than a line of dancers, The Experience fell back on 'Midnight Hour', 'Wild Thing' and other favourites from Jimi's Café Wha? repertoire, including 'Hey Joe', earmarked by Chandler as the début single. Though more "in the air" than actually popular in 1966, it was one of those ditties that never go away. It had already been recorded by the Byrds, the Leaves, the Standells, Tim Rose, the Music Machine, the Shadows of Night and less well-known US acts. Only the fast and staccato Byrds version—and an album track at that—had impressed itself even slightly on Britain's record-buying public. It was therefore near enough an ideal selection for launching The Experience.

'Hey Joe'

An unhurried arrangement by Tim Rose was the blueprint for The Experience's all-electric 'Hey Joe'. Noel's walking bass line, Mitch's rataplans and the careworn "aaaaaahs" of the Breakaways' female chorale underpinned the six-chord cycle

During their final UK tour, the Walker Brothers were sometimes upstaged by the supporting Jimi Hendrix Experience.

and crescendo bedrock for Jimi's menacing guitar obligato and solo, and his smoky delivery of the cowboy narrative.

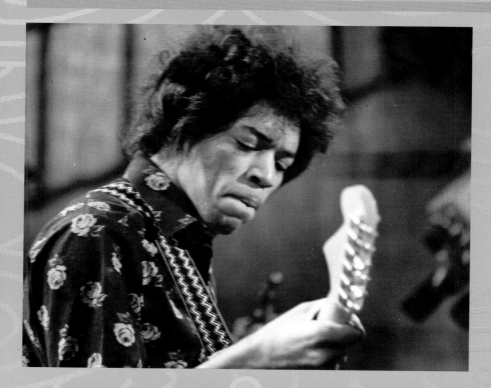

Wild Thing

"Here's a young man who could make a profound impression in the future!" raved UK paper *New Musical Express* after listening to a promotion

> ## "Here's a young man who could make a profound impression in the future!"
> *New Musical Express*

copy of 'Hey Joe' in December 1966. On the Friday before its release (on the 16th), an appearance on the last edition of *Ready Steady Go*, perhaps the most atmospheric UK TV pop magazine of the Sixties, was the first that Britain at large saw of Jimi Hendrix.

Far left: The Experience perform on British television for the first time, on *Ready Steady Go*.

Left: The Experience: (left to right) Noel, Jimi and Mitch.

> **"The roadies just touched those guitars, and there was instant feedback. Hendrix picked them up and the guitars made no noise at all— but if anyone else went near them, they just howled with feedback. He just knew exactly how to pick them up."**
>
> **Pearce Marchbank**

Jimi chats to UK vocalist Lulu—described by pop author Nik Cohn as "quite dreadful".

As well as the quality of the song to which he mimed, the visual impact of Jimi's bit with the teeth in the solo, and his and Noel's fuzzy haloes were more than sufficient to lift 'Hey Joe' off the runway. Its passage on to radio playing lists and subsequent climb up European Top 10s was further assisted by the application of all the usual undercover hype,

a sexy if gimmicky stage act, and Hendrix providing "good copy"—quirky wit uttered in a soft Yankee twang.

Accepted by all

An overnight sensation, Jimi captured the imagination of the British pop élite. Most important of all, he was the darling of female stars such as Marianne Faithfull, Lulu and Sandie Shaw. Though Sandie would describe him as "like an

exotic bird of paradise in crushed velvet plumage," beneath it all, they saw him as an innocent abroad, a little-boy-lost type who needed to be mothered.

Jimi with The Who. His favourite Who song was 'Boris the Spider' by John Entwistle (second from the left).

From the perspective of a different set of hormones, he was liked by many British guitarists, among them Rolling Stone Brian Jones, Dave Davies the youngest Kink, Ian Amey and John Dymond (alias "Tich" and "Beaky" in Dave Dee, Dozy, Beaky, Mick and Tich), Tony Hicks of the Hollies, the Spencer Davis Group's Steve Winwood, Peter Green from John Mayall's Bluesbreakers and, crucially, ex-Yardbird Jeff Beck. Like Hendrix at that point, the solos and riffs of these UK guitarists were constructed to integrate with the melodic and lyrical intent of each song rather than as a clenched teeth reaction to the intellectual and technical challenges of underlying chord sequences.

Master of feedback

Flashier guitarists like Eric Clapton of Cream and The Who's Pete Townshend were stunned by the newcomer's display of eclecticism and unpredictability in compatible

The Experience plug their début single, 'Hey Joe', on UK TV's Top of the Pops.

amounts. Equally fascinating was his mastery of barely explored possibilities of the electric guitar. Like Beck and Dave Davies, Hendrix had not dismissed guitar feedback as an irritating occupational hazard but had pursued it and similar distortions as aural effects, and methods of sustaining notes and reinforcing harmonics.

His mastery was illustrated in an observation by designer Pearce Marchbank, who was present at an Experience soundcheck in 1967. "The roadies just touched those guitars, and there was instant feedback. Hendrix picked them up and the guitars made no noise at all—but if anyone else went near them, they just howled with feedback. He just knew exactly how to pick them up."

An inspiration

Townshend and Clapton, reportedly, went to every Hendrix club engagement that winter, and Eric had his wavy locks tortured into Hendrix-Redding corkscrews. Both Cream and The Who had

Jimi himself wrote 'Purple Haze', The Experience's biggest UK smash of 1967.

much in common with The Experience, who also functioned without the almost compulsory rhythm guitar. Hendrix also acquired a taste for smashing up his equipment on

39

stage—"auto-destruction"—as pioneered by The Who. Hendrix's habit started during a booking in Munich in late 1966 when he capitalized on accidental damage to his guitar.

As well as developing the ideas of others, Hendrix roused unprecedented flair in the most

> ## "What he [Jimi] let Mitch Mitchell do on drums gave me space for what I wanted to do on drums."
>
> ### Robert Wyatt of the Soft Machine

disparate people. After catching him in action before the issue of 'Hey Joe', the Dave Dee group lent a pronounced Hendrix touch to 'Shame', B-side of 'Save Me', their Christmas chartbuster. According to Spencer Davis, his Group's 1967 US breakthrough, 'I'm A Man', was inspired by Hendrix, while Robert Wyatt attributed aspects of his experimentations with the Soft Machine to Jimi: "What he let Mitch Mitchell do on drums gave me space for what I wanted to do on drums."

Hendrix in the dressing room of London's Saville Theatre, January 31, 1967.

Of no less import was the view of UK blues enthusiast Peter Shertser, who saw Hendrix get the upper hand when sitting in with Cream at London University: "So he's come on, blown the place apart, Hendrix is getting all the ovations—from then on, I knew the guy was magic." Then there's an opinion given by a stranger who, during an Experience concert, sidled up to Beatle Paul McCartney and muttered, "You ought to get a bloke like that in your band, mate."

First London concerts
The London In Crowd's acceptance of The Experience meant that they were welcomed at about ten briefly fashionable watering holes. The Scotch of St James (within spitting distance of Buckingham Palace) and the Bag o' Nails off

Jimi wonders whether the British army will have him if this music lark fails.

Carnaby Street were the places to be after The Experience played their first two UK dates within their respective walls.

LSD—lysergic acid diethylamicide—had been "turning on" factions within London's beautiful people for almost a year before it was outlawed for recreational purposes in 1966. Its use had

> ## "So he's come on, blown the place apart, Hendrix is getting all the ovations—from then on, I knew the guy was magic."
> **Peter Shertser**

The Experience functioned without the almost compulsory rhythm guitar.

"You ought to get a bloke like that in your band, mate."

To Paul McCartney

Faces knew the drug well. So did ex-Animal Eric Burdon, Brian Jones and other cronies of Jimi, who probably first indulged in spring 1967. It reputedly set Jimi's psyche jumping with paranormal sensations and surreal perceptions that he trusted would carry him to untold heights of creativity—though those close to Jimi maintain that in those days he rarely took drugs, and never acid, unless a drink was spiked.

Hendrix at home

Guitar practice and serious composition were limited by space restrictions in transit and the laugh-a-minute novelty of one-nighters around the UK. Flashes of inspiration could only be explored fully in hotel room seclusion and backstage alcoves. Otherwise, song fragments born on his travels had to wait until he got back to his flat, in a tall Victorian block in the West End of London. With Keith Moon, John Lennon, Mama Cass and William Burroughs among other famous tenants before and after him, this

become so widespread that Dave Dee insisted to UK paper *Melody Maker* that, as far as the lads in his group were concerned, LSD still stood for pounds, shillings and pence, then the UK currency. The Pretty Things, Moody Blues and Small

one-bedroom apartment was sub-let to Jimi by lease-holder Ringo Starr. Visitors were often surprised at the sparse furnishings in a living room dominated by a television too near the fireplace and a large, expensive stereo system. As late as 1978, no one had yet stripped the place of the psychedelic décor that dated from Hendrix's stay.

It's a full life

As many callers discovered, Jimi still slept like the dead at the not unreasonable hour of four in

Jimi and Mama Cass were two of several famous tenants of lease-holder Ringo Starr's Montagu Square apartment.

the afternoon. Well, he was now leading what the economists would call a "full life". Driving, driving around the UK to strange towns and strange venues with more bookings than they could possibly keep. The Experience frequently had to drop everything to fit in photo calls, press interviews and radio or television transmissions.

One of the more intriguing of these was *Good Evening*, a UK TV chat show hosted by Jonathan King. The edition featured Mitch and his parents discussing how much Mr and Mrs Mitchell had become reconciled to the way their boy earned a living in the corrupt world of pop in the employ of wildman Hendrix. The foreseeable conclusion was the same stroke that everyone from Presley to the Pretty Things had pulled: that Jimi and his Experience were Nice Lads When You Got To Know Them.

In mid 1967, Jimi was on the way up, taking celebrity in his stride.

Onward and upward

They had reason to be nice, because 'Hey Joe' was proving to be an ignition point for continued advancement rather than a one-off signalling a drift back to obscurity. They all but eclipsed The Who headlining at London's Saville Theatre, in which Brian Epstein had a controlling interest. The Beatles' manager considered The Experience to be "the most talented act since the Rolling Stones". Thinking the same, Kit Lambert, The Who's manager, signed the trio to his Track Records. His investment was recouped promptly when the second Experience single, 'Purple Haze', stopped just short of topping the UK charts. Completing what was first regarded as a demo, the group had returned to the studio the following day to try to improve on 'Purple Haze'. Instead, they had second thoughts about

THE
Wild Thing

with no room for the long solos expected at club dates. So Jimi decided to awe the mob with naked sensationalism. Taking auto-destruction a step further during the 'Fire' finale, he torched his guitar, which he'd had the presence of mind to soak in petrol back in the dressing room.

Engelbert Humperdinck, Gary Walker, Cat Stevens and Jimi share a joke during the Walker Brothers tour.

On fire with the Walker Brothers

Engelbert Humperdinck was on the bill of The Experience's first UK tour on the "scream circuit" where they were contracted for two shows a night throughout April 1967. The main attraction was to be the Walker Brothers with Scott Engel, a vocalist with the range of a young Sinatra. The something-for-everybody fare was completed by Cat Stevens, newly transformed from folk-singer into a smartly attired pop idol, and Johnny B. Great and the Quotations, an ebullient sax-dominated combo.

For Hendrix, the jaunt got off to a doubtful start when he came close to being dropped from it altogether after the very first date at London's Finsbury Park Astoria. It had been estimated that there was time for The Experience to play only five songs—the two hits plus previews of 'Can You See Me', 'Fire' and 'Foxy Lady' from a planned début album—the previous session's rough-and-ready version—described as "ugly" (meant as a compliment) by Disc columnist Penny Valentine.

On the road with The Experience.

This publicity stunt—and flaunting of fire regulations—was gilded by other outrageous antics as Hendrix, clothed in eye-torturing colour, fell forward on his knees and rammed his instrument into his crotch while waggling his tongue suggestively.

Off-stage camaraderie

This proved too much for Britain's prudish provinces. The fretboard fireworks weren't repeated on this particular tour, but the other capers—moderated when necessary—became an established part of the act. Even Mick Jagger was moved to describe Hendrix as "the most sexual thing I've seen in a long time". It was not, however, without humour. After the teeth sequence one night, he spat out masticated fragments of seaside rock.

This jape may have been to amuse those watching from the wings. Despite the disparity of the cast, there was much offstage camaraderie. Jimi rarely missed opportunities to join in a jam, and Noel was always ready to deputize when Engelbert's regular guitarist was indisposed. There was much beery joviality in the artists' bar.

was a crude if uncluttered affair that thrived on musical interplay between its protagonists. Yet a more complicated approach might have emasculated its raw drive. Technically, it was almost purposely retrograde.

Finding a voice
Though touched up with vocal harmonies from Mitchell and Redding plus a pot-pourri of tambourines, handclaps and other percussion trifles, the album focuses almost exclusively on guitar, bass, drums and lead vocal, taped more or less "live". Among few special effects were an octave divider on 'Fire'; the varispeeded collage of spooky murmurings on quasi-instrumental 'Third Stone From The Sun'; and the alluringly enveloping sound of backwards guitar on the title track. Hendrix first heard this contrivance on the apposite "yawning" solo in 'I'm Only Sleeping' from 1966's *Revolver*

May 1967: The Experience relax in Jimi's flat, with two singles in the UK Top 20.

by the Beatles. If less related to the song melodically, this was improved on by Jimi as a technical accomplishment.

During his comprehensive shadowing of Chandler's production methods, Jimi asked whether studio trickery could doctor what he regarded as a dull voice. Yet, 'Third Stone from the Sun' excepted, it wasn't necessary. He was no Scott Engel but his singing had much improved since he had arrived in England. At a time when onstage vocal balance was still achieved by moving back and forth on the microphone, he'd got better at capitalizing on, rather than shrinking from, a limited vocal range. Rather than try and fail to hit top notes, he extemporized with the throaty crackle of a

soul singer, as can be heard on 'Fire', among other tracks.

Are you famous?

Even with the widespread critical and commercial success of *Are You Experienced?*, Jimi was still able to take celebrity in his stride, remaining pretty much his old amiable self. It was not unusual to hear stories of his politeness, like that from journalist Jo Cruikshank: "I was sitting at a table one night. I'd been off to dance, and Jimi Hendrix was sitting there, and I walked up and said, 'Sorry, this is my table'—and he was so polite and

In interviews, Jimi provided "good copy" in the form of a quirky wit delivered in a soft Yankee twang.

After playing the guitar with his teeth one night, Jimi spat out chewed-up fragments of seaside rock.

> **"I was sitting at a table one night. I'd been off to dance, and Jimi Hendrix was sitting there, and I walked up and said, 'Sorry, this is my table'—and he was so polite and apologetic— and I became a complete Hendrix fan after that."**
>
> **Jo Cruikshank, journalist**

apologetic—and I became a complete Hendrix fan after that."

At a Mothers of Invention concert at the Royal Albert Hall in 1967, Frank Zappa was singing 'Flower Punk', a send-up of 'Hey Joe', just as Jimi arrived. During the intermission, he ambled across the stage to say "hello" to his fellow Americans, and he grinned and waved in response to calls from the crowd. In hotel foyers, an amused Jimi would scribble in autograph books without precipitating public fuss—but

this wouldn't be the case for much longer. At the Aldershot stop of the Walker Brothers tour, for example, Redding and Mitchell drew the beginnings of a crowd when taking the air during the late afternoon rush-hour; even drawing attention to themselves, with Noel wearing the trousers and Mitch the jacket of the same eye-catching orange suit.

By contrast, Jimi didn't dare venture out in daylight. After the show, he was mobbed by libidinous females not much younger than himself. Pinned in a doorway, he lost tufts of hair to clawing hands while the other two bought their freedom with mere autographs.

Almost despite himself, Jimi was becoming a star. By 1968, the Hendrix frizz was common enough, even in English country towns. Nevertheless, neither Jimi nor his managers could yet assume that The Experience would be much more than a strictly European phenomenon like Cliff Richard and the Shadows, Dave Berry or Family. Released on Reprise, 'Hey Joe' had made no inroads into the *Billboard* Hot 100 chart in the US. Yet Chandler and Jeffery remained optimistic. After all, it was for the United States that The Experience had been designed. With their deepest musical roots in US culture, they were about to become an American group.

CHAPTER 3

The Hoochie Coochie Man

> In the late Sixties, most groups that carried any weight were operating ambiguously with experimental fancies on albums and tilting for hit singles with something in the same style but catchier.

In theory, The Experience were no exception with their second album, *Axis: Bold As Love*, and the follow-up to 'The Wind Cries Mary', 'The Burning Of The Midnight Lamp'. The latter, however, turned out to be a relative miss in Britain, and was relegated to a B-side in the States.

Reduced to the acid test of just voice and piano, it wasn't much of a song anyway. It lived chiefly in a riff in which a harpsichord was played in unison with a Stratocaster fed through a wah-wah pedal. This newish gadget was designed originally to make a guitar sound like a muted trumpet.

Wah-wah fading in and out of echo was but one detail of a production that seemed stratospheric on the pocket

transistors and monophonic record players that were standard for 1967's teenager. Yet, up against the unrefined gusto of, say, 'Purple Haze', 'The Burning Of The Midnight Lamp' was too pat, too dovetailed. As a result, not enough buyers could be blinded by science to push it far past the edge of the UK Top 20.

Axis: Bold As Love

Mediocre singles figures, however, were a surface indication of the respect accorded to The Experience by older album-buying adolescents, who were the core of the burgeoning market for "progressive" music. Unlike *Are You Experienced?*, *Axis: Bold As Love*—recorded in summer 1967—was intended as a complete work rather than a collection of individual items. Yet any one from around half the selections—say, 'Spanish Castle Magic', 'Little Wing' or 'You've Got Me Floating'—would have been a better single than 'The Burning Of The Midnight Lamp'.

A couple of pieces, none the less, defy adequate categorization and stood little chance of superseding 'Yesterday' as the most recorded song of

Left: Jimi at his usual place of employment.

Right: Axis: Bold As Love featured the most adept singing of Jimi's career.

55

all time. The album's opener, 'EXP', is pervaded by a spoof radio interview with an alien being (Jimi) and by noises not generally thought of as musical. Equally challenging is 'If Six Was Nine', which, though it had lyrics and a tune, is closer to 'EXP' than it is to 'Up From The Skies'.

Most of the tracks stand tall as straightforward songs, aided by perhaps the most adept singing of Hendrix's career. When required, he swerved cleanly from baritone to falsetto, and from mumbled trepidation to strident intensity.

Thinking in colours

Hendrix veiled some of the tracks in superficially thrilling special effects—most notably the fake effervescence of "phasing" on the 'Bold As Love' finale. "He would describe the sound he wanted in colours," explained Jack Kramer, one of Hendrix's custom device makers, "and sometimes it might be spatial. He said, 'I want to hear the sound of this underwater,' [so] I went to a local radio shop and bought two Styrofoam

Mitchell, Redding and Hendrix display their quiet good taste.

speakers—and I got a bucket of water, stuck them into the water with the wires on, and cranked up the volume. It sounded awful."

A vintage shot taken during Jimi's return to the States in 1967.

"He would describe the sound he wanted in colours, and sometimes it might be spatial. He said, 'I want to hear the sound of this underwater,' [so] I went to a local radio shop and bought two Styrofoam speakers—and I got a bucket of water, stuck them into the water with the wires on, and cranked up the volume. It sounded awful."

Jack Kramer, who made custom devices for Hendrix

Monterey

The fun and games of the *Axis: Bold As Love* sessions were interrupted by The Experience's first assault on North America. This began with a spot at an optimum moment—at Paul McCartney's insistence—during the International Pop Music Festival in Monterey, California on June 18, 1967. Arriving in his homeland five days beforehand, Jimi was struck by the unexpected joy of being a nobody again. It was, however, only a brief prelude to a large-scale and ultimately intolerable re-run of the British hysteria.

It started with a bang at the Monterey engagement, a few miles down the coast from the flower-power city of San Francisco, now as vital a pop Mecca for the US as Liverpool had been for the UK. So forceful was the publicity build-up that The Experience were billed above The Who, sitar virtuoso Ravi Shankar and even local lads the Grateful Dead. As the time crept closer, Jimi grew increasingly

Hendrix knocks 'em dead at Monterey, June 1967.

nervous that he might not live up to expectations. Introduced by Brian Jones as "the most exciting performer I've ever heard", he strode from the wings to a roar of welcome. A psychedelic Wild Man of Borneo, he was just what the hippy multitudes needed, dazzled as many of them were with chemically induced glimpses of the eternal.

Capturing America

Having become fully mobilized in Europe, his act was as staggering as it was ever going to get. Hendrix didn't spare any details. He did the splits, jack-knifed into the air, gnawed the strings and collapsed to his knees, streamlining all the outrages that were old hat back in London. The 'Wild Thing' finale crossed from the bucolic reality of the Troggs into a wilder dream than ever as Hendrix ravaged and sacrificed his guitar in a woomph of petrol, and then destroyed its amplification.

But it was not these excesses that frightened every guitarist in the audience; it was the confident

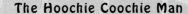

scope and imagination of Hendrix's playing, and Noel and Mitch's quick-witted responses. Virtually free-form—and even formless—at times, it was almost the sound at any given moment that

"The most exciting performer I've ever heard."
Brian Jones

counted, as The Experience rocketed far beyond the chords, rhythm patterns and rhymes of 'Foxy Lady', 'Like A Rolling Stone', 'Hey Joe' et al. Mistakes were shrugged off and arrangements blasted to pieces but, just when The Experience seemed to be lost, they'd establish eye contact and pull the song together again neatly within the space of a few bars. "Their appearance was magical," said Pete

The Hendrix magic: supreme show-manship and inspired soloing.

Johnson. "The way they looked, the way they performed and the way they sounded were light years away from anything anyone had ever seen before."

The USA was now Jimi's for the taking. The only hiccup was an ill-conceived and quickly aborted coast-to-coast trek supporting the Monkees, stars of a TV sit-com for which they had been created as America's answer to the Beatles. Each time The Experience played, their music was drowned as the pre-teen audience screamed for their idols to appear.

The Monkees headlined over The Experience for the ill-conceived US tour that followed Monterey.

Touring with the Floyd

In Britain, The Experience had peaked as chart contenders with *Are You Experienced?* and 'Purple Haze', but such a minor territory mattered little now, after playing to adulatory audiences on both coasts of the US. Nevertheless, their first bill-topping UK tour in November 1967 was a sell-out. Unlike the Engelbert/Walker Brothers package, the other artistes were of the same progressive stamp as Hendrix, because the divide between "rock"—which only the finest minds could appreciate—and vulgar "pop" had become such that mismatched pairings like Humperdinck and The Experience were no longer mutually beneficial.

As headliners, the group now had 40 minutes to strut their stuff compared to the eight each granted to small fry like the Outer Limits and Eire Apparent. The rest of the time was filled by The

> "Their appearance was magical; the way they looked, the way they performed and the way they sounded were light years away from anything anyone had ever seen before."
>
> Pete Johnson at Monterey

Move, Amen Corner, The Nice—and Pink Floyd.

The Floyd's biggest asset—and biggest liability—Syd Barrett was sardonically hailed as "laughing Syd" by Hendrix who, like other outsiders, was unaware that the charismatic Barrett was a desperately unhappy man. He was already proving

August 1967: The Experience return to London after conquering the USA.

THE
Jimi
HENDRIX
Experience

Jimi puts another crowd under his spell.

ill-equipped to deal with the intense demands of stardom, and was shortly to leave the Floyd. As intuitive if less polished a guitarist as Hendrix, Barrett was as prone to spontaneous improvisations that went beyond key and time signature, mixing severe dissonance and serene melody. Like Hendrix, he earned the esteem of Pete Townshend, Eric Clapton and others who wished they had the ability to be as adventurous.

The Fender Stratocaster

The Fender Stratocaster guitar that Hendrix played will be forever associated with both Jimi Hendrix and Hank B. Marvin of the Shadows—though it also gleamed under the string-calloused fingers of Ry Cooder, George Harrison, Eric Clapton and Burt Weedon. "It's got a tremendously sensuous shape, and it's very versatile," Hank enthused. "You can play any type of music on it."

Hendrix and Marvin both displayed generous employment of the tremolo arm—the note-

warping protrusion found on some electric guitars—and 'Throw Down A Line', Hank's 1969 single with Cliff Richard, featured Hank in Hendrix mode.

Jimi at the height of flower power.

End of an era

Now that Jimi had showed them how, other guitarists were managing the same in fêted "underground" venues. But at Christmas on Earth Continued, a night-long London spectacular, The Experience lorded it over the best of British psychedelic pop, including groups such as Pink Floyd, Tomorrow, The Move, Soft Machine, Traffic, the New Animals, the Graham Bond Organization, the Sam Gopal Dream, and Paper Blitz Tissue. This concert served as a final farewell to flower power in Britain, so *passé* by this time that it was already joke fodder for stand-up comedians.

Jimi in a blue mood.

It was almost a UK farewell to The Experience too. To the chagrin of their British following, the band were to be seen there only rarely as they concentrated on conquering the States.

The legend grows

When The Experience returned to the USA in the New Year for a schedule of nearly 50 dates, Jimi had become one of the most unthinkingly worshipped of rock guitarists at a time of growing respect for instrumental proficiency as the outlines dissolved between rock and jazz.

Instead of the swooning hysteria of the English tour, there was serious "appreciation" of guitar heroes like Hendrix, Jeff Beck, Alvin Lee—"the fastest guitar alive"—and Eric "God" Clapton, whose high-decibel Cream were now spinning out a three-verse blues for close on 20 minutes.

Like Cream, the Hendrix group racked up far greater achievements across the Atlantic than ever had been managed in the UK, breaking box-office records once held by the Beatles in Uncle Sam's baseball parks and winning awards in *Billboard* and *Rolling Stone*. Over Christmas 1968, Hendrix topped the US chart with the musical self-portrait *Electric Ladyland*.

The making of *Electric Ladyland*

Round-the-clock sessions for this double album took place at New York's Record Plant. As fame had granted him a more splendid certainty than

The Experience in Hollywood, February 1968.

before about everything he said and did, Jimi decided to produce the record himself—so almost anything went. Various members of The Move, the Walker Brothers and the Hollies had added icing to the *Axis: Bold As Love* cake, but now more auxiliary players than ever performed in increasingly significant roles.

Now that Hendrix was hot property in the US, a piece of *Electric Ladyland* action was not to be sniffed at, as Al Kooper, Larry Coryell and other top-notch guest musicians already knew. Often helpers were recruited simply because Jimi liked some facet of their personality. Two participants, Steve Winwood and Chris Wood, just happened to be loitering in New York after a Traffic tour. Nevertheless, it was what engineer Eddie Kramer described as the "tremendous influx of musicians that made the studio a breeding ground for creativity".

With a dollar sign hanging over every note, many tracks evolved in a manner that would seem to outsiders to be slap-dash. 'Voodoo Chile'—a sort of 'Hoochie Coochie Man' in orbit that occupied nearly one side of an album—developed from Muddy Waters' 'Catfish Blues' during a jam with Jimi, Mitch, organist Steve Winwood and, on bass, Jefferson Airplane's Jack Cassidy. Hendrix and Winwood earned over-dubbed stoned applause for inter-mingling obligatos; but more impressive is the segue from the cacophony following the requisite drum solo back into the 'Red House'-like structure.

During the recordings, Jimi would often unwind in the chic Scene Club a few blocks away. One evening there ended with an invitation to Dave Mason to the *Electric Ladyland* session that yielded The Experience's hit single version of Bob Dylan's 'All Along The Watchtower' from his austere, understated *John Wesley Harding* album.

Hendrix produces

Hendrix's tireless attention to console minutiae—stereo panning, editing, degrees of reverberation and so on—was laudable. Close-miked vocals floated effortlessly over layers of treated sound, whether thunderclap aggression or feathery emanations. Everyone from the lowliest tape-op to Jimi himself was on top form.

Electric Ladyland was, however, similar in style and content to its predecessor—and its raw materials were sometimes inconsequential and self-indulgent. Most of it couldn't hold a candle to *Are You Experienced?* The *Electric Ladyland* music was better; the songs weren't.

Though Jimi tackled the album's more oblique metaphysics without affectation, lyrically, many of his more offbeat lines seem too much like pretty-but-nothing syllables strung together to carry the melody. Other parts sound as if they were definitely put together while on LSD. Yet the outer space pseudo-mysticism was pretty standard in an age when Pink Floyd released 'Set The Controls For The Heart Of The Sun' and even the Troggs were singing about "the bamboo butterflies of yer mind".

In more direct addresses like 'Crosstown Traffic'—another of the spin-off hits—there are elements of frustrated eroticism. There was also controversy over the mildly pornographic UK sleeve photograph.

Family reunion

Two months after the release of *Electric Ladyland*, on February 12, The Experience were booked to play at Seattle's Center Arena. Jimi hadn't been

The Hoochie Coochie Man

Hendrix rocks and The Experience roll.

Money trouble

Immovable tours of Europe and North America halted the goings-on at the Record Plant temporarily, but no one could deny such work made a fortune for someone or other. Everyone in The Experience organization seemed happy with their cut—except the musicians. "Hendrix was not only one of the greatest musicians ever," observed Screaming Lord Sutch, "but one of the hardest done by. Though they [the group] were staying in the best hotels and could order anything they liked, they never actually had any money of their own."

With most of their earnings seemingly tied up, The Experience were obliged to borrow small amounts from menials—usually the road crew. Larger bills were settled through the office. Like many struggling artists abruptly rich, Jimi's consumption was more visible than those for whom wealth was second nature—like Mike Jeffery. Whenever the subject of money reared up, Jeffery tended to change the subject or find excuses for not parting with any. Jimi's previous lackadaisical glibness about finance now deferred to probing suspicion.

back to his home town or seen his family for nearly seven years—and he had a new stepmother to meet. Five months before, he had said to one interviewer that he was "scared to go home. My father is a very strict man." In the event, Jimi's whole family came to meet him at the airport and took him back home with them, and at the gig they sat in the front, Al proudly supporting his now famous son.

Any investigation of his manager's handling of affairs had to be put on hold as The Experience were either recording or on the move. Even "days off" were filled with interviews and photo sessions. If they saw little solid cash, they could cling to the irrefutable fact that now they were perhaps the highest-paid working band in the world.

Extended play

"Power trios" were popular in 1968, though, like Cream, The Experience, Blue Cheer and Rory Gallagher's Taste, most harked back to the Big Three's guitar-bass-drums Merseybeat test case. The most prevalent leaning was towards heavy blues—though The Experience were inclined to be more passionate

The mildly pornographic UK sleeve of *Electric Ladyland* was issued without Jimi's consent.

LIMITED EDITION BOX SET

THE JIMI HENDRIX EXPERIENCE **ELECTRIC LADYLAND**

"Hendrix was not only one of the greatest musicians ever, but one of the hardest done by. Though they [the group] were staying in the best hotels and could order anything they liked, they never actually had any money of their own."

Screaming Lord Sutch

Jimi under police escort after trashing a motel room during The Experience's Swedish tour in January 1968.

than coarse, surging to musical climaxes all the more rewarding for their controlled elegance.

As 1969 approached, however, any restraint or clever ironies became warped as the very vastness of the amphitheatres in which the bands played forced them to over-dramatize and exaggerate their act. The same impasse caused Cream's calculated disbandment in November 1968: in their "endless, meaningless solos," reflected Eric Clapton, "we were not indulging ourselves so much as our audiences—because that's what they wanted." The situation didn't change when Clapton joined the Blind Faith "supergroup" with Steve Winwood who, likewise, made the exasperated discovery that "we could play really terrible and get the same reaction as if we played good." In the same boat, Hendrix was extending four-minute numbers to half an hour on some occasions. As he toiled at the fretboard, snow-blinded US fans applauded clusters of bum notes as loudly as they did his most spellbinding moments.

Difficult fame

People were calling him a genius nowadays. But however much he warranted this dubious title, he was starting to wilt. Quite simply, he couldn't cope. Overworked and robbed of privacy by his adoring public, he was the subject of shabby paragraphs in the newspapers for incidents like his arrest in Sweden for trashing a hotel room when drunk. His name became synonymous with drug use. "I cleaned the place up, especially as I knew

Jimi backstage in London, preparing for another wild and wonderful show.

71

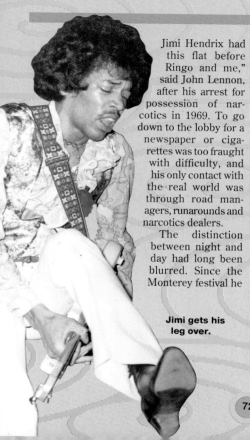

Jimi Hendrix had this flat before Ringo and me," said John Lennon, after his arrest for possession of narcotics in 1969. To go down to the lobby for a newspaper or cigarettes was too fraught with difficulty, and his only contact with the real world was through road managers, runarounds and narcotics dealers.

The distinction between night and day had long been blurred. Since the Monterey festival he

Jimi gets his leg over.

"I cleaned the place up, especially as I knew Jimi Hendrix had this flat before Ringo and me."

John Lennon, after his arrest for possession of narcotics in 1969

had caught only neon-lit glimpses of the places where a blinkered life had taken him. When asked what such-and-such a city had been like, he couldn't even find it on a map. What had been the point of travelling so far to gain souvenirs without wisdom, fatigue without stimulation, flattery without friendship?

Killing time

Like an insect, he could see only his immediate environment. In it, he sought comfort and creative stimulus via a greater intake of hard drugs and liaisons with groupies. In 1968, the top achievement for such girls was an orgasm at the thrust of "The Black Elvis". A Pink Floyd associate noticed that "the girls were throwing themselves at him like there was no tomorrow". Many realized that Jimi was not one to deny himself even the most fleeting erotic adventure. Time that hung

The Hoochie Coochie Man

heavy between one concert and the next wasn't killed only by practising guitar and board games. After visiting one venue on The Experience's second UK tour, agency assistant Melissa Chassay warned: "If you went backstage, there'd be a queue of girls waiting there. One by one, they'd go in and Jimi would fuck them...and, after an hour, he'd go onstage and tear the place apart."

Behind the mask

Jimi's brash outer shell was found to contain surprising gentleness, sensitivity and generosity. A *New Musical Express* article referred to his "sad Dylanish air", and he was once described as "the most charming, polite person in the entire world. If you went to his house, he took off your coat, that kind of thing." A touching image in an edition of *Disc* was of Jimi dressed up as Father Christmas at a children's party at London's Roundhouse. Furthermore, even as an international celebrity, he wasn't above a hush-hush show at one of his old high schools in Seattle.

Monika Dannemann, with whom Jimi was to spend the last few days of his life, claimed that she fell in love with him during their first, hour-long, conversation in January 1969, which she said revealed a gentle and considerate man rather

The Experience in customary subdued kit.

than the promiscuous drug-addict she had expected to find. It was Monika that Jimi often called when he felt in need of support; she hoped one day they would be married, but Jimi was too confused and ambivalent about his relationships with women ever to consider such a commitment in the 18 months that they knew each other.

If he had been a character in a happy-ending novel, the Jimi Hendrix saga could have ended there. He could have bested the villain and claimed the inheritance. Then he could have married a childhood sweetheart and settled down to a prosperous lassitude where nothing much was guaranteed to happen, year in, year out. Fiction aside, if he could have got what he was owed and retired at this point, at the age of 26, he could, indeed, have lived quite comfortably. Instead, he continued tramping the rock treadmill.

Opposite: **The peacock showing his feathers in his London flat.**

Below: **The image that scored smash hits.**

> "If you went backstage, there'd be a queue of girls waiting there. One by one, they'd go in and Jimi would fuck them...and, after an hour, he'd go onstage and tear the place apart."
> Melissa Chassay

Rancour in The Experience

With drug-sharpened paranoia about the management splitting his concentration, Hendrix's health and his standing within The Experience began

In the court of King Jimi: (left to right) Carl Wayne (The Move), Steve Winwood, Hendrix, John Mayall and Eric Burdon.

to deteriorate. A frustrated songwriter basking in a less intense limelight, Noel Redding's rancour at the neglect of The Experience's British audience was compounded by what he perceived as his leader's "unprofessional" behaviour, and this friction was manifesting itself in increasingly frequent flare-ups within the group. Through his own dogged persistence, compositions by Noel had been included on the last two albums. Under no commercial discipline to write more, his offerings were of less value to the group than the power he gave to Hendrix's swelling stockpile of numbers. "Jimi used Noel Redding songs as a token. He was a generous man. How else could 'She's So Fine' end up in the middle of *Axis: Bold As Love?*" said Alan Douglas.

> **"Jimi used Noel Redding songs as a token. He was a generous man. How else could 'She's So Fine' end up in the middle of *Axis: Bold As Love?*"**
> Alan Douglas

The Hoochie Coochie Man

A world-famous vocal-instrumental trio.

sound almost interchangeable on the occasions when they swopped instruments during jam sessions.

Diverging paths

Noel was by now emerging as quite a star in his own right. Cajoled into joining the Mothers of Invention in a comedy sketch at London's Royal Festival Hall in 1968, he was announced by Frank Zappa as "the formidable Mr Noel Redding" to a barrage of amused cheers. That summer, he'd formed a new group, Fat Mattress, with ex-members of the Loving Kind, initially as a vehicle to record his songs and allow him to revert to his preferred role as guitarist. With an eponymous début album nearly finished, Redding went so far as to suggest that his new group might be a suitable act to support Hendrix when he next went on tour.

But the concept that Noel merely cemented Hendrix's brilliance with rudimentary plonking had always been mistaken, as lead and bass guitars often merged in interlocking harmony. Over hundreds of hours onstage together, Jimi and Noel had learnt enough about each other to

Though Fat Mattress did, indeed, open the show during a 1969 tour of the United States, Noel Redding's tenure with The Experience was coming to a close—but then so was The Experience itself.

CHAPTER 4

The Star-Spangled Banner

"Revolution is this year's flower power" —so Frank Zappa summed up in 1968.

With President Nixon's war in Indo-China as the common denominator, kaftans had been moth balled. Their former wearers were now attending genuinely explosive anti-war demonstrations and student sit-ins in protest against what George Harrison of the then disintegrating Beatles called "all these old fools who are governing us and bombing us and doing all that".

When asked about Vietnam and other inflammable topics, Jimi Hendrix was hip enough to understand that killing people is wrong. He wouldn't—as Mick Jagger did—join with militant protesters outside the US Embassy in London. Yet he was as forward in supporting pacifism verbally, albeit in a detached, sweeping, pop-starrish fashion: "It's best to have violence on stage and watch it through TV than do it yourself." Words are cheap after all. Sometimes, however, the ex-paratrooper's ingrained respect for the profession of arms would show, in spite of himself. An instant pundit with no time for tact, he assured one interviewer that "after China takes over the whole world, then the whole world will know why America's trying so hard in Vietnam."

A radio station in the Deep South was twice firebombed for its radical anti-war policy. At the same time, airplay

> **"It's best to have violence on stage and watch it through TV than do it yourself."**
> Jimi Hendrix

problems with what had once been classified as "race" music was an important aspect of the US colour problem that reached one of its many turning-points in 1968. To white extremists, negroes as slaves had been cattle. Free and human, they were a nuisance—undesirable and embarrassing. Especially so were the more uppity ones like Martin Luther King.

Jimi, music and racism

After this noted black spokesman for civil rights was slain by a white sniper on April 4, 1968, Hendrix, a known admirer, dedicated a lengthy and untitled instrumental lament to King the following evening during an Experience show in a predominantly black district of Newark, New Jersey. Though the audience was, as usual,

Jimi tops the bill at the Isle of Wight Festival, August 1970.

Above: The final days of The Experience—and the strain is beginning to tell.

Opposite: If it's Thursday, it must be Minnesota.

almost entirely white, this gesture precipitated pressure on Jimi to side with the newly founded Black Panthers and similar violent factions who—pre-empting rap—barked boorish revolutionary rhetoric while sporting coshes, flick-knives, pistols and other weaponry as "self-protection" against white opposite numbers.

Star-spangled protest

When cornered by an aggressively friendly "brother", Jimi felt uncomfortable. Outwardly affable to avoid losing a fan, he'd catch the eyes of his entourage, wondering whether it was OK to exchange anything beyond a side-stepping smile. How much safer it was to hedge his bets by being non-doctrinal while articulating east-west-black-white views in the occasional all-purpose number acceptable to the counter-culture. Into the bargain, he incorporated an arrangement of 'The Star-Spangled Banner' into the stage act. It was a harrowing us-versus-them overhaul of the US national anthem, but not an original notion. A vocal version by José Feliciano had been released earlier in 1968. However, when Radio Hanoi began broadcasting to US troops in Vietnam three years later, it opened with the Hendrix rather than the Feliciano treatment.

Jimi had also assisted on recording sessions by the Ghetto Fighters and the Last Poets. The

The Star-Spangled Banner

obscurity of these US outfits allowed them to be less guarded when discussing socio-political activism in song.

Finally, there was no direct message from Jimi Hendrix to the Black Panthers. It invited too much trouble. After Martin Luther King, he might be the next famous black to die a hero's public death. With so many regarding him as more than just an entertainer, the possibility of his onstage slaughter was sufficient reason to cut back on concerts to concentrate on the foundation of his own Electric Ladyland recording complex in New York.

Individual expression

As the auxiliary musicians used on the album of the same name had already indicated, Jimi was frustrated by the limitations of a fixed set-up. This now extended to stage work too. He wasn't alone. "We feel that today's scene is moving very much away from permanent groups and more towards recognition for individual musicians," pontificated Steve Winwood, in the royal plural, to *Melody Maker*, "The trend is going more in the direction of the jazz scene when musicians

Jimi jams with (left to right) Eric Burdon, Mitch Mitchell, Jack Cassidy (Jefferson Airplane) and Buddy Miles.

just jam together as they please." The finale of a Buddy Miles Express concert in an LA club during the summer had been an amalgam of Miles, organist Graham Bond, Eric Burdon and The Experience. An incurable "blower", Jimi—with and without Noel and Mitch—was now taking part in all sorts of onstage and studio jams with musicians of every type and ability.

Going through the motions
The period that led to the break-up of The Experience was one of creative stagnation and indecision for Jimi. Jamming was the line of least resistance. Occasionally he would drop everything to develop some flash of musical inspiration. But, after strumming a bit, all the fragments of song would seem

By 1969, The Experience were in huge demand—yet they were beginning to break up.

the same to him, just vibrations dangling in the air. Glazed languor would set in, and his mind would drift off anywhere but back to the job in hand. Maybe he'd try again tomorrow.

Jimi's audience knew him now largely by hearsay and press rumours that often painted him in nearly the same psychotic hues as Syd Barrett, Pink Floyd's lost leader, soon to be extinguished artistically. Yet as Sixties myths rather than mere mortals, both Barrett and Hendrix were made to last. By this time, however, they were last year's models. In the ascendant was the "high energy" blues-plagiarized brutality of Led Zeppelin, Ten Years After, Grand Funk Railroad and Black Sabbath, whose guitar heroes—Jimmy Page, Alvin Lee and all the rest—were homing in on the most gut-wrenching aspects of the Hendrix blueprint.

Prisoner of his past

Honouring existing contracts, The Experience worked the same circuit for the first half of 1969. As it was with Jeff Beck, Hendrix was revered as a leader of a form he was coming to despise. A prisoner of his past, he would slouch on to unacknowledged acclamation by an unduly patient audience waiting for him to go through the whole pointless ritual again. On cue, he'd plunge into the sex-man routine with his guitar like a

Diddle-iddle-iddle-iddle-iddle-iddle-iddle...

In 1969, Billy Cox, Jimi's old army pal, enlisted with the Band of Gypsys.

magician reproducing a popular effect to amuse children. In between, there were long moments of standing glumly still. For devilment, he'd slam out deliberate dischords or brew up ear-splitting feedback. But most of the fun had gone now. The highlight of the day wasn't the show any more but the building up and winding down.

Messing with the law

On top of it all was too-plain evidence that, fretboard messiah or no, Hendrix wasn't above the law. On May 3 he was arrested at Toronto International Airport for possession of controlled drugs—critically, a quantity of heroin discovered in his flight bag. If guilty, he faced years in jail. When the case came up seven worrying months later, the soberly dressed defendant sought to convince the jury that it was all a dreadful mistake. As he had often admitted to drug abuse in unrueful print, Jimi could only be contrite about the bad old days. Somehow he left the Canadian courthouse with a character unblemished by a felony conviction.

His old habits were resumed immediately. Even between bust and trial, he'd continued to imbibe hallucinogenics as carelessly as alcohol in the backstage torpor that passed the time during the tour that ended with the final Experience concert somewhere in America on June 29, 1969.

Gypsy Sons and Rainbows

While Noel Redding flew back to London and Fat Mattress, Mitch Mitchell was held over for the next Hendrix venture. Mitch and Jimi had always got on well together; Mitch always felt completely comfortable in Jimi's company. As well

In 1969, Jimi was revered as a leader of a musical form he was coming to despise.

as being gentle and soft-spoken, Jimi seems to have been completely open and frank. If something bothered him, he would say so right away, rather than brood on any problems.

Rehearsals took place on a farm in Woodstock, just over the New York State border from Canada. This was at the invitation of its owner, Juma Sultan, who'd known Hendrix when he was Jimmy James. Despite a command of several orchestral instruments, Sultan chose to thump congas. With the recruitment of another hand-drummer, Jerry Velez, the project was to have a pronounced percussive emphasis. However, its core was Jimi, Mitch and two old pals from the King Kasuals era. Bass player Billy Cox was still living in Tennessee when he got a call from Jimi during the last weeks of The Experience. Through Billy, contact was then made with Larry Lee, a guitarist whom both had known and liked back in Nashville.

The "Black Elvis" inflames his audience.

Jimi and his new group, Gypsy Sons and Rainbows, appeared only once in public, in August 1969, at the Woodstock Music and Art Fair—now seen as the zenith of hippy culture.

Stealing the show at Woodstock in 1969.

Woodstock

After a lot of hanging about, Hendrix and his boys closed the festival in the grey of a cold Monday morning. Straggling and loose, the set—a continuous musical performance—seemed as if it could fall to bits at any second. For most, however, it was enough that Jimi appeared at all.

Hendrix rode 'em down at Woodstock by linking old favourites like 'Voodoo Chile' and less inspired material with instrumental rambles. The high point was a 'Star-Spangled Banner', captured for all time on the tie-in triple album and movie. Screaming from a lone guitar, it was interpreted generally as a wordless vote of no confidence by the nation's youth in square old President Nixon and the rest of George Harrison's "old fools who are governing us". As John Sebastian said during his own slot, it was "just so far out, man".

At New York's Madison Square Garden with The Experience as storm clouds gather.

The beginning of the end

From then on it was downhill all the way. Woodstock was the Jimi Hendrix moment, never to return. Even if he was suffering from a writer's block, no time would have been better for making a financial killing with a world tour. Perhaps renewed confidence and concrete new ideas might have come from it. Instead, Hendrix marked time as the uneasy focal point of the Band of Gypsys, originally called Sky Church. An all-American and all-black trio of Jimi, Billy and Buddy Miles, it may have been one of Jimi's irresolute attempts to placate black militants. He sported what was called an "African natural" haircut, and included in the set such songs as 'Power Of Soul' and 'Machine Gun' rather than falling back on more joyous crowd-pleasers from The Experience portfolio.

Sections of 'Machine Gun' sounded just like one during the outfit's first show—at New York's Fillmore East on New Year's Eve 1969—where Jimi dedicated it to "the soldiers fighting in Chicago, Milwaukee, New York and Vietnam". The set also included a seasonal medley of 'Little Drummer Boy' and

'Auld Lang Syne', played 'Star-Spangled Banner' style. It was noticed that his virtuoso performance was less theatrical and not so concerned with embellishing numbers with gratuitous frills. Yet, though many critics agreed that he might have begun to "get it together" again, less than a month later, he made a final and dramatic onstage exit from the Band of Gypsys after only two numbers at a charity show at Madison Square Garden.

The US issue in spring 1970 of an album of the Fillmore recital was followed by talk of a reunion with the original Experience. On paper, it made sense: Jimi was at a loose end after the Gypsys, and Mitch had remained essentially a free agent since Woodstock. Both were still on friendly terms with Noel, whose Fat Mattress had made another album, and great things were expected of a spin-off single 'Naturally'.

Hendrix plays his upside-down Fender Stratocaster with the sure touch of a genius in May 1969.

Falling star

With Redding sticking with hitless Fat Mattress, Jimi began a European tour backed by Mitchell and Billy Cox. During this trek, he materialized in England like a ghost at the end of August for the third Isle of Wight festival. As it had been at Woodstock, it was raining lightly, and the

**The composer whose songs still merit
revivals in the 1990s.**

man, I can't play this guitar...' The sleeves were
too big and got in the
way of the strings. He
was about to go on, and
his trousers split."

Eventually, he reached
the central microphone
in garments hastily
repaired and customized
by Dexter and Margaret
Redding, Noel's mother.
By previous standards,
it was a listless perfor-
mance, punctuated with
fuddled, almost apolo-
getic announcements
through a faulty PA sys-
tem. Margaret and Jeff
watched anxiously as
more impetus was lost
while Jimi spent endless centuries tuning up.
While he fought to get a grip on himself, a few
scattered boos rent the air. Yet most onlookers
wanted to like him, fretting when he flagged and
cheering when he rallied.

He was, wrote one reviewer, "at the end of his
tether". For all the months striving for a new direction in block-booked studios, onstage he was still

proceedings were over-running into the small
hours. Jimi himself contributed to the delay
when, as compère Jeff Dexter recalled, "it took
him about forty minutes to get himself together.
He went to go on in his new gear and said, 'Hey,

treated like a vendor of entertainment. Any subtle silences and pianissimos risked being undercut by outbreaks of stamping, whistling and, worst of all, bawled requests for the good old songs like 'Wild Thing' and 'Purple Haze'.

Isle of Fehmarn

Much the same situation prevailed a week later, at an even more dismal event on the Isle of Fehmarn in Denmark. Though billed as a "Love and Peace Festival", discomfited snarls signified a murderous mood as fans grappled for both a good view and shelter from the heavy rain and freezing temperatures.

Part of the Hendrix set was filmed for posterity. This was to gain historic importance, as it turned out to be his last public performance. Jimi went the distance to the customary encore, then smiled, waved and vanished into the wings for ever. He wouldn't have thought so, but perhaps running through his best-loved songs on this forlorn back-of-beyond stage might not have been such an unfitting place to finish after all.

Jimi gets real, real gone.

Round the next corner

The blending of pop star grandeur and hip sensibility kept Hendrix's head above water financially—but there was always the disturbing psychological undertow, summarized by another travelling man, Dave Berry: "The thing about this business is that you never know what's waiting round the next corner". Johnny Kidd, killed in a road accident, didn't—nor did Buddy Holly and Otis Redding. Hendrix had recently been interviewed by

Hendrix, along with Jimmy Page, Frank Zappa and Jeff Beck, was one of the most adventurous electric guitarists of the century..

Jazz veteran Miles Davis discussed a musical merger with Hendrix in 1970.

Merger with Miles?

Miles Davis—another Isle of Wight attraction—and his arranger Gil Evans had discussed a musical merger with Hendrix, who had jammed already with the jazz trumpeter's English sidemen, guitarist John McLaughlin and bass player Dave Holland. In transition from jazz to a strata of pop categorized as "jazz-rock", there were signs too that Davis—the proverbial "oldest teenager in the business"—had lent a thoughtful ear to Hendrix.

Miles's 1970 double album, *Bitches Brew*, was as much a fixture in university rooms as the familiar poster of Che Guevara—or a dog-eared *Electric Ladyland*. Nothing since had been as huge a smash for Hendrix. Despite the approbation of Davis, Roland Kirk and other highbrow musicians, his income still hinged on mundane day-to-day record sales. In an industry where chart positions are arbiters of success, there were perceptible signs of commercial danger for Jimi as the Seventies moved into gear.

UK's *Melody Maker,* in which he'd spoken of forming a big band, like Frank Zappa's Mothers of Invention, using a method of conducting peculiar to himself. There'd be a guitar around his neck, but it wouldn't be as vitally cohesive as in The Experience or Band of Gypsys—more like a front-line horn in a jazz combo. What was jazz after all? "A lot of horns and top-speed bass lines," answered Jimi. "Most of those cats are playing nothing but blues."

If a return to previous prominence could never be ruled out, Reprise and Track were then considering themselves lucky to have milked him when they did. Some really amazing stroke had to be pulled to get him back on his perch again,

95

"He was the heaviest doper I ever met."
Eric Burdon

as he'd long lost the knack of writing or picking even 'Crosstown Traffic'-sized hits. Nevertheless, an occurrence shortly before 1970's pre-Christmas sell-in got under way gave Hendrix's investors a miracle.

Last hours

On Wednesday September 16, Jimi "sat in" with Eric Burdon's War, then resident at London's Ronnie Scott's club, and played superbly. It was Burdon who once described Hendrix as "the heaviest doper I ever met", which was about to be proved unfortunately accurate.

Left: Breaking down the walls of heartache.

Right: During his last months, Jimi applied a brake to much of his onstage swagger.

Monika Dannemann, Hendrix's German girlfriend, was present when he died. In December 1993, the case was re-opened.

Accounts given of Jimi's movements that night differ, though both Chas Chandler and Alan Douglas recalled long discussions with Jimi about new projects and albums, and meetings were arranged for further discussions. Jimi spent Thursday with Monika Dannemann, and it was arranged that he should turn up at the Speakeasy to jam with Mitch and Sly Stone. He never turned up—an unusual thing for Jimi, who never missed a jam. Instead he went to a party, returning in the early hours of Friday morning. Monika recalls that they talked through the night, falling asleep around dawn. Later that morning, she woke and went to get some cigarettes. When she returned, she saw that he had been sick and had taken some of her sleeping pills. She couldn't wake him, so called first his doctor and then an ambulance. She was too late.

Eric Burdon reckoned that his friend had written a suicide note but no one else has ever seen it—and Burdon later admitted to being stoned when he made this claim. The London coroner was to settle for an open verdict, as although the cause of death was confirmed to be inhalation of vomit due to barbiturate intoxication, it could

not be established whether Jimi had deliberately or accidentally overdosed, as it was the combination of drugs and alcohol rather than the amount that caused the intoxication.

Whatever the cause, James Marshall Hendrix was pronounced dead on arrival at St Mary Abbot's Hospital in Kensington on Friday September 18, 1970. John Marsh, Pink Floyd's light-show operator, spoke for many when he said: "The 1960s ended for me when they announced on the radio that Jimi Hendrix was dead."

Jimi in fashionable Victorian military jacket, London 1967.

CHAPTER 5

The Things I Used To Do

From Buddy Holly's smash with 'It Doesn't Matter Any More' in 1959, it was understood that death can revive a sagging chart career.

Before they'd even wiped away the tears, music business moguls would be compelled to meet demand kindled by tragedy by rush-releasing product while the corpse was still warm. So it was that a single of 'Voodoo Chile (Slight Return)' was lifted by

A single of 'Voodoo Chile (Slight Return)' was lifted by Track from *Electric Ladyland* to soar to Number 1 in the UK within weeks of Jimi's funeral.

Track from *Electric Ladyland* to soar to Number 1 in the UK within weeks of Jimi's funeral and burial at Greenwood Cemetery, Washington, after a star-studded funeral service. Next, *The Cry Of Love* came close to topping album charts on both sides of the Atlantic. The following year, *Hendrix In The West* and *War Heroes* made lesser chart incursions—but made the charts all the same.

Other entrepreneurs began pondering what Hendrix product they'd be entitled to issue too. An apparently insatiable—

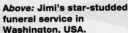

A*bove:* Jimi's star-studded funeral service in Washington, USA.

***Opposite:* The end of an era: Greenwood Cemetery, September 1970.**

The first posthumous album, *The Cry Of Love*, came close to topping album lists on both sides of the Atlantic.

Left: **The man, the myth, the magic.**

and uncritical—appetite for the late Jimi on disc was to be exploited fully in the 300-odd albums with him as chief selling-point that have been marketed since 1970. Noel Redding underestimated the lengths to which people would go when he pointed out, "They are taking something like £40-60 million a year, but they haven't got that much stuff left now." As late as 1988, previously unheard tapes were still being unearthed in dusty spools and rushed to the pressing plant.

Scraping the barrel

If documentary rather than recreational, some such as *Isle Of Wight* were intriguing. But, despite grandiose titles like *The Eternal Fire Of Jimi Hendrix* and *Jimi Hendrix At His Best*, most were either musical mistakes or items on which Jimi barely figured at all. In any event, they were never intended for public

One of 300-odd albums with Hendrix as chief selling-point that have been put on the market since 1970.

> ## "He was a virtuoso, but his music was dangerous and, despite its familiarity, it still is— and that, I reckon, is the mark of greatness."
> ### Nick Saloman of the Bevis Frond

consumption. Usually, they showcased little more than indolent improvisations round twelve-bar blues, two-chord riffs and similar digressions.

The most barrel-scraping examples reveal superimposition of posthumous backing tracks and even applause on to the sketchiest demos. Yet there are enough Hendrix worshippers around to make such exercises worthwhile. For these diehards, nothing on which he ever breathed is too insignificant to be interesting.

If the truth were told, *The Band Of Gypsys, The Cry Of*

> ## "They are taking something like £40-60 million a year, but they haven't got that much stuff left now."
> **Noel Redding**

Love and his contribution to the Woodstock soundtrack—all officially approved by Jimi—had been dismissed mostly as consolidation rather than development of the *Are You Experienced?* and *Axis: Bold As Love* blueprints—though they've all had rave notices since the wave of international grief gave tracks such as 'Angel' (from *The Cry Of Love*) a lasting piquancy and "beautiful sadness".

The Jimi Hendrix Memorial Foundation

In the course of time, complicated but fixed financial channels were established whereby Jimi's assorted and incoming royalties found their way to Al Hendrix, his father and sole heir. Through Al came the setting-up of The Jimi Hendrix Memorial Foundation in 1971. Its purpose was to award five music scholarships every

Al Hendrix during his famous son's induction into the 1992 Rock 'N' Roll Hall of Fame at New York's Waldorf Astoria.

year to talented youngsters in Washington State.

It was oddly appropriate that, thanks to Jimi, these boys and girls should be sweating over Chopin. Though their spectral patron had his share of young men's vices, muckrakers remain hard-pressed to ravage a distinguished, charitable, gentle and humorous man who had realized some extraordinary visions as a musician. "Why isn't Jimi Hendrix regarded as one of the century's great composers...like John Cage?" asked electronics boffin Brian Eno in 1989. "He is somebody who defined the way people think about music [but] you mustn't be popular, because anyone that's popular automatically can't possibly be interesting musically."

The Hendrix songbook

However much he might have broken musical barricades *per se*,

Jimi composing on his guitar in Hawaii in 1968.

Jimi as a pop composer was no Gershwin. Yet a wide range of artists dipped into the Hendrix songbook. Of his contemporaries, Rod Stewart reached the UK Top 10 with 'Angel' in 1972 while 'Little Wing' was in Eric Clapton's stage act from 1970, and was selected for the souvenir album of his 1974 "comeback" bash at London's Rainbow theatre. Jimi may have been more flattered, however, by Bob Dylan's use in concert of the *Electric Ladyland* arrangement of 'All Along The Watchtower'.

The next decade brought 'Castles Made Of Sand' by up-and-coming folk rocker Mark T, and 'Are You Experienced?' by both Devo and the Magic Mushroom Band, paladins of the "new psychedelia". Jimi also left a mark on New Age music through

Left: **Marianne Faithfull, Twinkle and Sandie Shaw were as struck by Jimi's looks as any of his less well-known female fans.**

Right: **Jimi, the focus of the spotlight in 1969.**

Left: In 1986, lookalike Phil Lynott of Thin Lizzy was under consideration for the title role in a proposed bio-pic about Hendrix, but died of a drug overdose a few months later.

Previous pages: Jimi and Mitch plug their album in Honolulu in 1968, in one of a series of radio interviews.

instrumental revivals of 'The Wind Cries Mary' and 'Purple Haze' from Symbiosis and the Kronos Quartet respectively. Sharing the same opinion about Hendrix as Brian Eno, the latter were led by David Harrington, also a son of Seattle, which by the 1990s had become a centre for grunge/hardcore groups like SubPop, Nirvana and Mudhoney, whose collective style, however hamfisted and excessive, is traceable to the one who first put their city on the cultural map.

Borrowing Hendrix style

Of older rock musicians, Detroit's Ted Nugent was one of several guitarists who borrowed the most abrasive facets of Hendrix's musical style and stage act to become a reliable draw at openair gatherings in the mid Seventies. Another was England's Robin Trower. He acknowledged his artistic debt by the ritual placing of a photograph of Hendrix on top of his amplifier at every performance. Before he formed his own trio,

The Things I Used To Do

Trower's Hendrix foibles had become incompatible with the music of his previous group, Procol Harum, who, nevertheless, paid homage to his idol in 1971's 'Song Of A Dreamer'.

John Mayall's 'Accidental Suicide' was more a cautionary tale than a tribute—and, though Steve Stills's début solo album was dedicated to Jimi alone, it was extended to Duane Allman and Canned Heat's Alan Wilson on a 1973 Stills track, 'Blues Man'. Even Bob Marley, another Hendrix fan, hired guitarist Junior Marvin for the Wailers because he "thought he could hear a streak of Hendrix in Junior".

Jimi lived on to varying degrees in all manner of diverse sounds. As well as those who properly absorbed aspects of Hendrix as part of the development of an idiosyncratic style, there were also blatant copyists, from the Purple Fox—who approximated Jimi's hits on a Seventies budget LP—to a more recent illusionist, Seattle's own Randy Hansen, whose booking fees are known to rise during the week either side of Jimi's birthday and September 18.

Jimi relaxes backstage, April 1967.

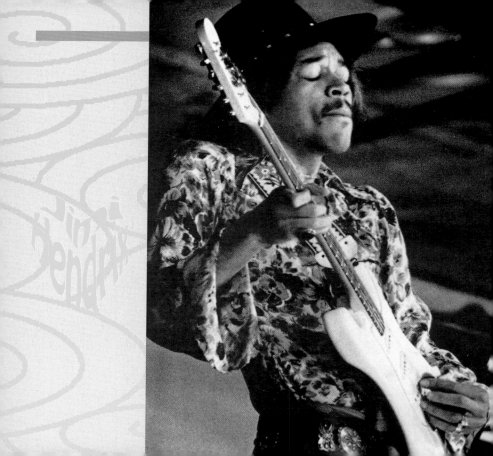

Electric genius

If he'd lived, there's every reason to suppose that Jimi would still have been making records in his old age, albeit at a pace involving long periods of vanishing from the public eye. One journalist had described Hendrix as "a young Satchmo with sharp fangs and a phallic ax". As it was, he never got the chance to show that he was less in the rock 'n' roll tradition than next in an innovative line stretching from Louis Armstrong to John Coltrane to Miles Davis. While it's possible to speculate for ever on what might have been, what is indisputable is that Jimi Hendrix endures as the name most often brought up whenever modern electric guitarists are discussed, and is the yardstick by which they will always be judged.

James Marshall Hendrix (1942–1970).

Chronology

(Includes significant record releases.)

1942
November 27   Johnny Allen Hendrix born in Seattle, USA to Al and Lucille Hendrix.

1946
September 11   Johnny Allen Hendrix is renamed James Marshall Hendrix.

1951
December 17   Parents divorce. Father gets custody of Jimmy and his brothers.

1958
February 2   Mother dies in Seattle.

1959
Jimmy plays his first official engagement as guitarist; joins the Rocking Kings as bass guitarist before transferring to lead.

1960
Leaves school. Joins Thomas and the Tomcats.

1961
May 31   Enlists in US army.

1962
January   Forms the King Kasuals with a line-up that includes fellow soldier and future Band of Gypsys member Billy Cox on bass guitar.

July 2   Discharged from army.

1963
March   Joins all-purpose backing group for

numerous trans-continental package tours headlined by the likes of Jackie Wilson, the Supremes, Slim Harpo and Little Richard.

1964

Bases himself in New York City where he is hired as backing guitarist to the Isley Brothers.

1965

January	Joins Little Richard's band, the Upsetters.
October	Joins Curtis Knight and the Squires.

1966

November–May	Works with Joey Dee and the Starliters, King Curtis, Carl Holmes and his Commanders and others as well as Curtis Knight's outfit.
July	Forms his own group, Jimmy James and the Blue Flames, for club residencies in New York's Greenwich Village, where he is "discovered" by Chas Chandler.
September 23	Flies to London, where he and manager Chandler form The Jimi Hendrix Experience.
October 13	Concert début of The Jimi Hendrix Experience.
December 16	UK release of 'Hey Joe'.

1967

March 17	UK release of 'Purple Haze'.
May 5	UK release of 'The Wind Cries Mary'.
May 12	UK release of *Are You Experienced?*
June 18	The Experience perform at the International Pop Music Festival, Monterey, California.
August 14	US release of *Are You Experienced?*
August 19	UK release of 'The Burning Of The Midnight Lamp'.
December 1	UK release of *Axis: Bold As Love*.

Chronology

1968

January	US release of *Axis: Bold As Love*.
April	UK release of *Smash Hits*.
October	*Electric Ladyland* released simultaneously in the UK and US. UK release of 'All Along The Watchtower'.
November 18	US release of 'Crosstown Traffic'.

1969

April 4	UK release of 'Crosstown Traffic'.
April 11	Start of third North American tour.
May 3	Hendrix's arrest for possession of controlled drugs at Toronto International Airport.
June 29	Final Experience concert.
July	US release of *Smash Hits*.
August 18	Hendrix performs Woodstock Music and Art Fair, Bethel, New York.
December 10	Acquitted of drugs charges at Toronto Court House.
December 31	Début concert of Band of Gypsys.

1970

January 28	Final Band of Gypsys concert.
April	US release of *Band Of Gypsys*, and start of North American tour by Hendrix, with members of both The Experience and Band of Gypsys.
June 12	UK release of *Band Of Gypsys*.
August 31	Hendrix and US tour group top the bill at Isle of Wight Festival.
September 6	Hendrix's final official concert on the Isle of Fehmarn, Denmark.
September 18	Pronounced dead on arrival at St. Mary Abbot's Hospital, London.
September 28	London inquest records open verdict.
October 1	Burial at Greenwood Cemetery, Renton, Washington, USA
October 23	UK release of 'Voodoo Chile'

Discography

Albums

Are You Experienced?
May 1967
UK: Polydor 847234-2
US: Warner 6261
Chart position: UK 2, US 5

Axis: Bold As Love
December 1967
UK: Polydor 847243-2
US: Warner 6281
Chart position: UK 5, US 3

Smash Hits
April 1968
UK: Polydor 825255-2
US: Warner 2276
Chart position: UK 4, US 6

Electric Ladyland
October 1968
UK: Polydor 847233-2
US: Reprise 6307
Chart position: UK 6, US 1

Band Of Gypsys
April 1970
UK: Polydor 847237-2
Chart position: UK 6, US 5

Woodstock
June 1970
US: Atlantic SD 500-2

At the Monterey Pop Festival
September 1970
UK: ITM960008
Chart positions: UK-, US 16

The Cry Of Love
March 1971
UK: Polydor 847242-2
US: Warner 2034
Chart position: UK 2, US 3

Woodstock Two
April 1971
US: Atlantic 781 981-2

Experience (soundtrack)
August 1971
UK: Bulldog BDCD-40023
Chart position: UK9, US -

Isle Of Wight
November 1971
UK: Polydor 847236-2
Chart position: UK 17, US?

War Heroes
October 1972
UK: Polydor 847262-2
Chart position: UK 23, US 48

Jimi Hendrix
March 1975
Available on import
Chart position: UK 35, US -

Crash Landing
March 1975
UK: Polydor 847263-2
US: Warner 2204
Chart position: UK 35, US 5

Woke Up This Morning and Found Myself Dead
October 1980
UK: RLCD 0068
US:Red Lightnin' 68

Last Experience (his final show)
1980s
UK: Zeta ZET-517
US: CD-42

The Jimi Hendrix Concerts (Live '68-'70)
August 1982
UK: Castle CCSCD-235
US: Reprise 22306
Chart position: UK 16, US 79

Singles Album
February 1983
Available on import
Chart position: UK 77, US -

Kiss The Sky
October 1984
UK: Polydor 847261-2
US: Warner 25119
Chart position: UK -, US 148

Jimi Plays Monterey (soundtrack)
February 1986
UK: Polydor 847244-2
US: Reprise 25358
Chart position: UK -, US 192

Live At Winterland
May 1987
UK: Polydor 847238-2
US: Ryko RCD-20038
Chart position: UK -, US 11

Sixteen Greatest Classics
1988
UK: Big Time 261525-2
US: Big Time 2615252

Radio One
November 1988
UK: Castle CCSCD-212
US: Ryko RCD-20078
Chart position: UK 30, US 119

Variations On A Theme
November 1989
US: HL00660040

The Essential Vols.1 & 2
November 1989
US: Warner 26035

Cornerstones '67-'70 (Best Of)
October 1990
UK: Polydor 847231-2

Lifelines (The Jimi Hendrix Story)
May 1991
US: Warner 26435
Chart position: UK -, US 174

Isle of Wight
February 1991
UK: Polydor 847 236-2

Stages (in-concert box set)
February 1992
UK: Polydor 511763-2
US: Warner 26732

The Ultimate Experience
November 1992
UK: Polydor 517235-2
US: MCA 10829
Chart position: UK 25, US 72

Free Spirit
UK: Thunderbolt CDTB-094
US: Magnum 94

Gold Collection
UK: Deja 2 D2CD-03

Graffitti Collection
UK: Graffitti GRCD-13

His Final Live Performance
UK: Pulsar PULS 003

New York Session
UK: Trad Line TL-1301

Night Life
UK: Thunderbolt CDTB-075
US: Magnum 75

Purple Haze (early recordings)
Available on import

Voodoo Chile
Available on import

Singles

'Hey Joe'
December 1966
Chart position: UK 6, US -

'Purple Haze'
March 1967
Chart position: UK 3, US 65

'The Wind Cries Mary'
May 1967
Chart position: UK 6, US 65

'The Burning Of The Midnight Lamp'
August 1967
Chart position: UK 18, US 20

'All Along The Watchtower'
September 1968
Chart position: UK 5, US 20

'Crosstown Traffic'
November 1968
Chart position: UK 37, US 52

'Voodoo Chile'
October 23, 1970
Chart position: UK 1, US -

'Freedom'
March 1971
Chart position: UK -, US 59

'Gypsy Eyes'
October 1971
Chart position: UK 35, US -

'Dolly Dagger'
October 1971
Chart position: UK -, US 74

'Johnny B Goode'
January 1972
Chart position: UK 35, US -

Day Tripper
November 1988
Chart position: UK - , US -

Jimi Plays Berkeley
October 1991
Chart position: UK -, US -

Index